CRAFTING WITH DUCT TAPE: EVEN MORE PROJECTS

Written and Illustrated by Kathleen Petelinsek

CHERRY LAKE PUBLISHING • ANN ARBOR, MICHIGAN

CHERRY LAKE Publishing

Published in the United States of America by Cherry Lake Publishing
Ann Arbor, Michigan
www.cherrylakepublishing.com

Photo Credits: Page 4, ©Songquan Deng/Shutterstock; page 5,
©Garsya/Shutterstock; page 6, ©Photodiem/Shutterstock; page 7,
©Maria Dryfhout/Shutterstock; page 29, ©LesPalenik/Shutterstock
Copyright ©2016 by Cherry Lake Publishing

Library of Congress Cataloging-in-Publication Data
Petelinsek, Kathleen, author, illustrator.
Crafting with duct tape : even more projects / Written and Illustrated by
Kathleen Petelinsek.
pages cm. — (How-to library. Crafts)
Summary: "Follow along with these fun, creative projects to create a variety
of useful or decorative objects using duct tape." — Provided by publisher.
Audience: Grades 4 to 6
Includes bibliographical references and index.
ISBN 978-1-63362-374-3 (lib. bdg.) — ISBN 978-1-63362-402-3 (pbk.)
— ISBN 978-1-63362-430-6 (pdf) — ISBN 978-1-63362-458-0 (ebook)
1. Duct tape—Juvenile literature. 2. Tape craft—Juvenile literature. 3.
Handicraft—Juvenile literature. I. Title.

TS198.3.A3P48 2015
745.5—dc23   2015005399

Cherry Lake Publishing would like to acknowledge the work of the
Partnership for 21st Century Skills. Please visit *www.p21.org* for
more information.

Printed in the United States of America
Corporate Graphics
July 2015

TABLE OF CONTENTS

Duck, Duct, Tape

Duct tape has been used for everything from basic home repairs to major construction projects.

Have you ever used **duct** tape before? In the early 1900s, this useful tape was called "duck tape" because it was made from cotton duck cloth. The original tape wasn't sticky like it is today, either. It was simply a long strip of cotton duck cloth. Strips of duck tape were used to make shoes stronger and to decorate clothing. In 1902, duck tape was even used in the construction of the Brooklyn Bridge.

Although there were several sticky tapes available in the early 1900s, **adhesive** backing wasn't added to duck cloth strips until 1943. That year, a woman whose sons were fighting in World War II was worried that the ammunition boxes issued by the U.S. government would cause problems for the soldiers. She wrote to President Franklin D. Roosevelt with the idea of sealing the boxes with a fabric tape that the soldiers could easily use. The president liked her idea, and the tape was produced in an olive drab color for the army. Soldiers used the new tape not only for the ammunition boxes, but also to repair their weapons and jeeps.

After the war ended in 1945, the tape was sold in hardware stores. It was used to wrap air ducts and given the name duct tape. With the new name came a new silver color to match the ducts themselves. Today, duct tape is still produced in this silver gray color, but it also comes in a wide variety of colors and patterns. Its uses are almost limitless!

Stores sell many different colors of duct tape.

Basic Duct Tape Tools

As you may have guessed, you will need duct tape to make the crafts in this book. Duct tape can be purchased from hardware and department stores. It comes in a 2-inch (5 centimeters) width and 0.75-inch (2 cm) width. The crafts in this book all use 2-inch (5 cm) tape. You can use a single color to complete the projects, but choosing a few different colors or patterns is a great way to personalize your creations.

Tools

- **Scissors or craft knife:** Duct tape is made out of fabric. As its original inventor intended, it can be torn by hand. However, you will need scissors or a craft knife if you want a more **precise** edge. Craft knives are sharp, so always ask an adult for help if you use one.

- **Cutting mat or waxed paper and painter's tape:**
  You will need a cutting mat to protect your work surface
  when using a craft knife. A cutting mat is also helpful
  when you need to put the sticky side of the tape down
  while making your item. The cutting mat is designed so
  the sticky tape can easily be peeled off. If you don't have
  a cutting mat, you can lay down waxed paper and tape
  it in place with painter's tape.

- **Ruler:** A ruler will help you measure pieces of tape for
  your projects.

- **Low-temperature glue gun:** Many
  of the crafts in this book require a
  glue gun. A low-temperature glue gun
  is the safest kind to use. Always ask
  an adult to help you when using the
  glue gun. Even low-temperature glue
  guns can get quite hot.

Mark It!

Mark your place in the book you are reading, or make these bookmarks as presents for your friends and family. This is a great first project because the basic techniques used to make these bookmarks are used in other projects as well.

Materials
- Duct tape (any color or pattern)
- Ruler
- Scissors
- Cardstock
- Hole punch
- 4-inch (10 cm) piece of thin ribbon

Steps
1. Measure and cut two 4-inch (10 cm) strips of duct tape.
2. Measure and cut a 1.5-inch (3.8 cm) by 3-inch (7.6 cm) piece of cardstock.
3. Lay one strip of tape on your work surface, sticky side up.
4. Carefully place the piece of cardstock in the center of the tape.

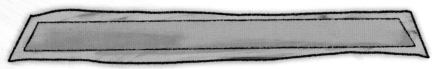

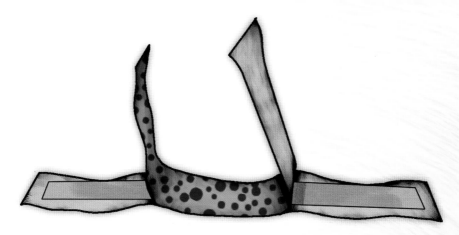

5. Place the other strip of tape, sticky side down, on top of the first strip and cardstock. Stick everything together by touching the centers of the two strips together. Line them up as best you can, then gradually work the pieces together all the way to each end. Flatten the strips with your hands to push any air bubbles out.

6. Cut off the corners of one of the ends of the bookmark. Trim the top edge.

7. On the same end where you cut off the corners, punch a hole near the center of the bookmark.

8. Fold the ribbon in half, then thread the looped end through the punched hole. Thread the loose ends through the loop and pull them tight.

9. Trim any loose bits of tape from the bottom edge of the bookmark.

Duct-Toppers

Give your pencils a little personality by attaching some duct tape characters to them.

Materials for Hair, Face, and Clothes

- Duct tape (2 solid colors and 1 patterned tape)
- Ruler
- Scissors
- Pencil
- Low-temperature glue gun
- Googly eyes
- Thin permanent markers (red and black)

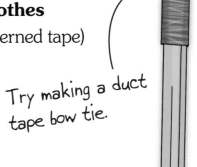

Try making a duct tape bow tie.

Steps

Fringe Hair

1. Measure and cut a 2-inch (5 cm) piece of solid-colored duct tape. Lay the tape sticky side up on your work surface. Fold over one of the 2-inch (5 cm) sides so it leaves about 0.25 inches (6 millimeters) of adhesive showing. Use your scissors to cut slits into the folded edge of the tape. Stop the cuts short at the point where the adhesive is still showing.
2. Wrap the fringed tape around the eraser end of your pencil. The fringes should stick up beyond the pencil.

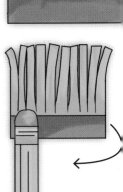

TIP: You can cut the tape into a hat or any other shape.

Clown Hair

1. Measure and cut a 3-inch (7.6 cm) piece of solid-colored tape. Lay the tape sticky side up on your work surface. Place a pencil on one of the short ends of the tape so the metal part that holds the eraser to the pencil sticks to the tape.

2. Fold the tape in half by bringing the other short end of the tape to the eraser end of the pencil and sticking it to the metal piece. Press the tape together, sealing the eraser end of the pencil inside the folded tape.

3. Use your scissors or ask an adult to help use a craft knife to shape the square tape into clown hair.

Face and Clothes

1. Measure and cut a 0.75-inch (2 cm) piece of solid-colored tape. Wrap the tape around the pencil, overlapping the bottom edge of the hair.

2. Measure and cut a 2-inch (5 cm) piece of patterned tape for your topper's clothes. Wrap it around the pencil, overlapping the bottom edge of the face color.

3. Ask an adult to help you attach the googly eyes to your topper's face using the glue gun.

4. Use the thin permanent markers to draw a nose and mouth on the face of your pencil topper.

TIP: Glue a small pom-pom in place for a clown nose.

Classy Key Chain

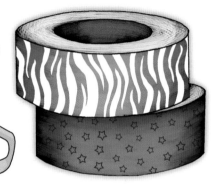

Carry the keys to your school locker or bike lock with you by clipping this key chain to a handy spot on your backpack. Make key chains for your parents and they will never lose their car or house keys in their bags again!

Materials

- Duct tape (one or two colors or patterns)
- Scissors
- Ruler
- Key ring
- Simple metal spring snap hook

Steps

1. Measure and cut a 6-inch (15 cm) piece of duct tape. Fold the tape in half lengthwise, sticking it together so that you have a long, narrow strip of tape with no adhesive showing.
2. Put the strip through the key ring and fold it in half. The key ring should rest at the fold.

TIP: You can purchase a key ring and simple metal spring snap hook from a jewelry, craft, or art supply store.

3. Measure and cut a 3-inch (7.6 cm) piece of tape. (If you are using two colors of tape, cut this piece from the second color.) Cut this piece in half lengthwise. You should now have two pieces of tape that each measure 3 inches (7.6 cm) by 1 inch (2.5 cm).

4. Wrap one of the thin strips of tape around the folded longer strip to secure the key ring in place at the fold. Set the other thin strip aside for step 8. Now that the key ring is secure, trim the loose ends of the folded long strip to make sure they are even.

5. Measure and cut a 1-inch (2.5 cm) piece of tape of any color. Fold it in half lengthwise. Stick it together so there is no adhesive showing. Put this strip through the hook and fold it in half. The hook should rest in the fold.

6. Use the piece of tape you set aside in step 4 to attach the hook's loose ends of tape to the loose ends of the key ring piece. You should end up with a long piece that has a hook on one end and a key ring on the other.

TIP: Make a longer version of this project to form a leash for your dog or cat. If you have a really big dog, you might want to use extra duct tape to make the leash stronger!

Fancy Flowers

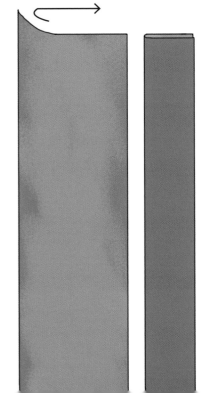

These colorful flowers are great for decorating shoes, notebooks, hats, and purses. They are also used to make the 3-D Masterpiece (see pages 20–21) and Festive Wreath (see page 22) projects.

Daisy Materials

- Duct tape (1 to 6 different colors)
- Scissors
- Ruler
- Stapler
- Large, flat button
- Low-temperature glue gun

TIP: To make a larger flower, start with longer strips. To make a smaller flower, start with shorter strips.

Daisy Steps

1. Measure and cut six 10-inch (25 cm) strips of duct tape. Place them on your work surface sticky side up. You can use all the same colors or all different colors.

2. Fold each piece of tape in half lengthwise, sticking it to itself. You should end up with six long, narrow strips of tape with no adhesive showing.

3. Place one piece of tape **perpendicular** across a second piece of tape to form a cross. Staple the two pieces together in the middle. Repeat this with the remaining pieces of tape. You will have three crosses when you are done.

4. Line up the crosses on top of each other so they form an **asterisk** shape. Staple them together in the middle. Trim the ends of the shape to make them even, if needed.

5. Fold each of the ends to the center. Staple them together in the center of the asterisk shape. You will have 12 loops.

6. Cut a slit down the center of each loop, stopping near the center of the asterisk shape. There should now be 24 loops sticking out around the center of the shape.

7. Ask an adult to help you attach the button to the center of the flower using the glue gun.

8. Glue the flower to a headband, handbag, or notebook.

Petunia Materials

- Duct tape (2 colors)
- Ruler
- Scissors

Petunia Steps

1. Measure and cut a 12-inch (30.5 cm) piece of duct tape for the center of the flower.
2. Fold it lengthwise, leaving about 0.25 inches (6 mm) of adhesive showing.
3. Use scissors to snip fringe into the strip (see Fringe Hair on page 12 for instructions).
4. Starting at one end of the tape, roll the fringe together. This will be the center of your flower.
5. Cut eight pieces, each 4 inches (10 cm) long, from the second color of duct tape. These will be your petals.
6. Fold one of the pieces in half widthwise, leaving about 0.25 inches (6 mm) of adhesive showing. Use your scissors to round off the folded edge of the tape. Repeat for the remaining seven pieces of tape.
7. Take one of the petals you just created and stick it to the base of the center of the flower.

8.   Stick the second petal to the base, overlapping the first by about half the width of the tape.

9.   Repeat until all eight pieces are stuck to your flower.

10. Fold the petals down a little to open the flower up.

Carnation Materials

- Duct tape
- Scissors
- Ruler

Carnation Steps

1. Measure and cut an 18-inch (45.7 cm) piece of duct tape.

2. Fold it lengthwise, leaving about 0.25 inches (6 mm) of adhesive showing.

3. Start rolling one end of the tape, sticking it to itself with the adhesive you left showing.

4. Once you have rolled about 1 inch (2.5 cm), start to gather up the tape as you roll. This will create a fuller shape. Be careful not to gather too much at a time or the flower will not hold together. Continue gathering and sticking as you roll. Once you are done, you will have a simple carnation.

TIP: If you would like a flower with a stem, wrap the center of the flower around a pipe cleaner.

Creating a 3-D Masterpiece

This masterpiece is created using the flowers from the previous activity. You can use flowers that are all the same color or a variety of different ones. Match up different color combinations to create a custom piece of art for any room.

Materials

- Old newspapers
- Canvas (the larger the canvas you use, the more flowers you will need)
- Paint
- Paintbrush
- Sketchbook and pencil
- Many different Fancy Flowers (see pages 16–19)
- Scissors
- Ruler
- Low-temperature glue gun
- Green duct tape

Steps

1. Spread newspapers out over your work surface to protect it. Paint the canvas with

the color of your choice so it is covered completely, including the edges. Use a light blue to create a sky background. Dark green or even black will make the colorful flowers pop off the canvas. Let the paint dry before moving on to the next step.

2. Think about what you would like your masterpiece to look like. Sketch your vision.

3. Arrange your flowers on the canvas to match your sketch.

4. Once you have flowers arranged the way you like, ask an adult to help you attach them to the canvas using a glue gun.

5. To add stems to your flowers, cut thin strips of green duct tape and stick them to the canvas.

6. To make a leaf, fold a 6-inch (15 cm) length of green tape the short way. Cut points on both ends of the tape to form it into a leaf shape. Glue it to your canvas. Add as many leaves as you like.

Festive Wreath

Hang this wreath from your front door at Christmas, Valentine's Day, or any other time you feel like celebrating. You could even use orange and black tape to make a spooky wreath for Halloween!

Materials

- 12-inch (30.5 cm) foam wreath
- Duct tape
- 100 carnations (page 19)
- Low-temperature glue gun

TIP: You can use a variety of Fancy Flowers (see pages 16–19) to decorate your wreath. Make a different one for every holiday!

Steps

1. Wrap the entire foam wreath with duct tape by winding the tape around and around. Overlap the tape with itself as you wrap. This will help you make sure the entire wreath is covered. If you miss a spot, simply tape over it with a smaller piece.

2. You will need about 100 carnations to cover the entire wreath. Ask an adult to help you attach the carnations to the wreath using the glue gun. Make more carnations if you have space to fill.

Jewelry Frame

You can make this frame any size you like.
A long, narrow frame is great for necklaces.
Smaller frames work well for earrings.

Materials

- Two foam cores, 15 inches (38 cm) by 20 inches (51 cm) each
- Ruler
- Pencil
- Cutting mat
- Craft knife
- Duct tape (any color or pattern)
- Scissors
- 12-inch (30.5 cm) by 17-inch (43 cm) screen
- 6-inch (15 cm) picture-hanging wire
- Metal paper clips

Steps

1. Measure 2 inches (5 cm) from any edge of one of the pieces of foam core and mark it in two spots along the edge. Use a ruler to draw a line connecting the two marks. The line should be **parallel** to the edge of the foam core,

reaching from edge to edge. Repeat for the other three sides of the foam core. When you are done, you should have a box drawn on your foam core that measures 11 inches (28 cm) by 16 inches (40.6 cm).

2. Place the foam core on the cutting mat. Ask an adult to help you cut the box you just drew from the inside of the foam core. Using your ruler as a straight edge to cut along, use the craft knife to slice the box out of the foam core. The remaining foam core should now look like a picture frame.

3. Place the picture frame piece on top of the second piece of foam core. Trace the box you just cut onto the uncut piece. Make sure the two pieces line up with each other exactly.

4. Ask an adult to help you cut the box shape out of the second piece of foam core, turning it into another frame.

5. Cover each of the frame shapes with duct tape. One way to do this is to wrap the frames like you did for the Festive Wreath (see page 22). You can also simply cut pieces of tape to match the lengths of the frame sides. Then cut pieces to fold around each of the outside and inside edges of the frame.

Choose different colors and patterns to create a unique look.

6. After both frames are covered in tape, choose the side that looks best to be the front of your jewelry frame. Place this side down on your work surface so the back is facing up. Set the other frame piece aside.

7. Center the screen on top of the frame piece. Once it is in position, tape it to the back of the frame. Make sure the screen is **taut** as you tape it in place.

8. Place the second frame on top of the first one. The screen should be sandwiched between the two frame pieces.

9. Tape the outer edges of the frame pieces together.

10. Tape each end of the picture-hanging wire to the top of the backside of your frame. Ask an adult to help hang your frame on the wall.

11. Hang dangly earrings by poking them through the screen. Unbend paper clips to form S shapes, poke them through the screen, and hang necklaces and bracelets from them.

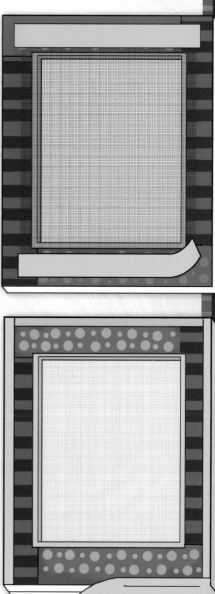

Duct Tape Basket

Start out by making this small, simple basket. Once you have the basic idea, you will be able to make baskets of any size and shape! Change the colors to match different rooms.

Materials

- Duct tape (2 or 3 colors or patterns)
- Scissors
- Ruler
- Painter's tape

Steps

1. Measure and cut six 10-inch (25.4 cm) pieces of duct tape that are all the same color.
2. Fold each of the six strips in half lengthwise. Trim any sticky adhesive from any of the edges.
3. Tape three of the strips to your work surface using painter's tape. Line them up so they are even and right next to each other.
4. Weave one strip through the three strips taped to the table starting 2.5 inches (6.4 cm) down from the top.
5. Weave a second strip into the three strips taped to the table. The second strip should be tight against the first strip.

6. Weave the last strip through the taped strips.
7. Secure the weave by taping a 2-inch (5 cm) square of tape over the center of the woven piece. This is the bottom of your basket.
8. Cut two 14-inch (35.5 cm) strips of tape. (If you are using two or three colors, cut them from the second color.) Fold the strips in half lengthwise. Trim any sticky adhesive edges from the strips. These strips will form the sides of your basket.
9. Place one of these strips below the last woven strip on the bottom of your basket to continue the weaving pattern. Tape the edge of it in place. Weave the first side strip through the three taped strips.
10. Begin the second side strip below what you just wove, continuing the woven pattern.
11. Secure the first side of weaving with a 2-inch (5 cm) square piece of tape, just like you secured the bottom side.

Glossary

adhesive (ad-HEE-siv) a substance, such as glue, that makes things stick together

asterisk (AS-tuh-risk) the mark (*) used in printing and writing to tell readers to look elsewhere on the page for more information

duct (DUHKT) a tube that carries air or liquid from one place to another

parallel (PAR-uh-lel) staying the same distance from each other and never crossing or meeting

perpendicular (pur-puhn-DIK-yuh-lur) at right angles to another line or to a surface

precise (pri-SISE) very accurate or exact

taut (TAWT) stretched tight

For More Information

Books

Bell-Rehwoldt, Sheri. *The Kids' Guide to Duct Tape Projects.* Mankato, MN: Capstone Press, 2012.

Dobson, Jolie. *The Duct Tape Book.* Richmond Hill, ON: Firefly Books, 2012.

Morgan, Richela Fabian. *Tape It and Make It: 101 Duct Tape Activities.* Hauppauge, NY: Barron's, 2012.

Rau, Dana Meachen. *Crafting with Duct Tape.* Ann Arbor, MI: Cherry Lake Publishing, 2013.

Web Sites

Duck Tape Club—Ducktivities

http://duckbrand.com/duck-tape-club/ducktivities

Find and share ideas for making crafts, clothes, and other creations with duct tape.

Exploratorium

www.exploratorium.edu

This museum's Web site encourages curious thinkers and creators.

Index

About the Author

Kathleen Petelinsek is a children's book author, illustrator, and designer. As a child, she spent her summers drawing and painting. She still loves to do the same today, but now all her artwork is done on the computer. When she isn't working on her computer, she can be found outside swimming, biking, running, or playing in the Minnesota snow.